I keep coming out

Bonsai Cp

I keep coming out

one woman's **message of hope**

Bonsai Cox

I Keep Coming Out

Copyright © 2013 by **Bonsai Cox**

Cover and book design by Cory Freeman
Hawk photo by Bonsai Cox

Printed in the United States of America

The Troy Book Makers • Troy, New York •
thetroybookmakers.com

To order additional copies of this title, contact your favorite local bookstore or visit www.tbmbooks.com

ISBN: 978-1-61468-192-2

If you judge people,

you have no time to love them.

-*Mother Teresa*

It never stops.

It will never stop.

I just keep coming out.

Out to family, new friends, people at work, strangers.

Or I make a choice to not come out.

Maybe this is true for you, too.

～～～～～～～～～～～～～～～

Being gay is just a part of me.

A part of me I've been aware of for 50 years. Why does the word "gay" scare some people off? It's just a word, a word with 3 letters, a word with two meanings. Gay means happy. And gay can mean being lesbian or homosexual.

When I was four years old, my mom experienced me as "the little man of the house", something she told me 40 years later. I have no idea what gave her this sense about me. Maybe it was because I was attentive, always there? Because I was a little "tomboy"? Or was my mother seeing a difference between my identical twin and me? That one of us was gay and the other was straight?

I have fun with the words gay and straight. The opposite of straight is crooked. Since I'm gay, not straight, the first thing that comes to mind is: "Oh, I must be crooked!"

Like gay, crooked also has several meanings. It might mean that something's not right, not good enough, a description full of judgment, which is so far from my truth about being gay. Or a crooked path meandering through the woods might lead you toward adventure, new discoveries. Maybe that straight line has breaks in it.

I just keep coming out.
I just keep coming out of that closet.

The culture back 50 years ago wasn't ripe with diversity. Sometimes I felt pressure from others to stay in the closet. They might have said or thought: "Don't make any fuss, be quiet, maybe it will go away, maybe you will outgrow being gay".

Out of sight, out of mind.
Or, to put it another way: now you see me, now you don't.

And then there was the workplace. I could have been fired from work if they knew that I was gay. I'm reminded of the "Monday morning pronouns" phenomenon. Like most others in the closet then, I would use the word "he" in place of "she", so that my co-workers would think that I was dating the opposite sex. This lying resulted in successfully misleading others, but sometimes I wasn't able to remember what I had told one person or another.

~~~~~~~~~~~~~~~~~~~~~~~~~~~

This was confusing to say the least, and I
didn't feel good about myself. I regretted that I
couldn't be honest with them. I lied because I
felt it wasn't safe to tell them. And when I did,
I would worry about who they might speak to,
and where "the information" would end up.

I wasn't out to myself for a long time.

Others knew it, or at least they thought that I was gay. I was 22 years old when I entered my first relationship in 1964. And then it had to be hidden from everyone, protected.

I could be outed before I admitted to myself that I was gay, or was ready to actually say the words "I'm gay" to someone else.

I was taken aback when, sometime in the 70's, a female friend who was close to me and my partner, found out one day that we were "gay".

Neither of us ever saw her again.

I still find it shocking that this friend could disown me in a split second. I was still the same person after my "gayness" was acknowledged. I was still lovable, worthy and fun.

I would have loved to have had a conversation with her. I have no way of tracking her down. I don't even know if she's alive, or what she might say about her experience.

I wonder if she ever thinks about the two of us she walked away from back then, or what she thinks about gay people now.

I thought that we were friends.

It still stings.

There were a number of years that I feared that my parents would disown me if I told them that I was gay.

Could they just walk away as if I didn't exist, too?

Could they shun me, or forget who I was prior to coming out?

That didn't happen.
While they never approved my choice to come out, they eventually accepted it.

And how about that closet?

I keep coming out of **what?**

A closet with a door. I could disappear by shutting the door, so as not to be seen.

~~~~~~

How did I ever survive that closet?

There was a time when I was more comfortable in there. It was familiar.

I could hide from myself and from others.

Sometimes, I might have stayed in the shadows of the closet. I could duck back in if necessary. I might have leaned against the door, and looked out. But carrying that closet around was very burdensome.

Heavy little fellow.

Once out in the light, I could breathe freer and more easily.

I was more alive.

~~~~~~~~~~~~~~~~~~~~~~

When I came out to someone, I wondered,
would there be a shift in their perception of me?

Would this new information make a difference?

Would something change now that they knew
something more about me? What were my
motives for sharing this? Would I take that risk?

Was it a risk?

Would it be freeing for me, or for them, or for
both of us?

Sometimes I imagine this "closet" as invisible.
It's a cultural construct, not an essential part of me.

It's what I make of it that's important.

～～～～～～～～～～～～～～～

I can be surrounded by my own imagination.

That closet can be very small or as expansive as I want it to be. I can take myself out of the closet or put myself back in.

The closet may always be there.

I just don't have to use it.

I'll always be gay, always be coming out.

I'll continue to meet new people on a daily basis.
I'll continue to make choices about whether to
let this one or that one stand in the light with me.

It's just the way it is right now.

There are so many more options today.

Back in the 60's, we couldn't imagine this freedom. Although this freedom is limited at times, it's beginning to spread its wings and take flight.

Now we can be more open about the person we are with. We can walk hand in hand with our partner in some places, get married, and celebrate our pronouns.

I'm thankful for family, friends and co-workers who love and like me.

I feel good about myself.

I hope to continue to be curious, adventurous and inspiring.

Please know, whether you're gay or straight, that you are extraordinary and special.

You will face challenges and become stronger for it.

Be resilient.

Take good care of yourself.

May you find your wings